Poetry for Young People

William Butler Yeats

Edited by Jonathan Allison
Illustrated by Glenn Harrington

Sterling Publishing Co., Inc.
New York

Acknowledgments

I am very grateful to Sheila Anne Barry at Sterling for her help and encouragement. Deepest thanks to my wife, Anna, and to the following: George Bornstein, Enoch Brater, Kerry Fried, Janez Gorenc, Sam McCready, Judy McGowan, Jackie Nugent, Ronald Schuchard, and George Watson.

Dedicated to Victor and Philip

—Jonathan

To Chris, Evan, and Sean—
A hint of heaven is in our dance on the stone house floor under the little green plastic hats.

—Glenn

Photograph of William Butler Yeats on page 4. From the copy in The Rare Book Collection, The University of North Carolina at Chapel Hill.

"The Second Coming" is reprinted with the permission of Scribner, an imprint of Simon & Schuster Adult Publishing Group, from *The Complete Works of W. B. Yeats: Volume I, The Poems, Revised*, edited by Richard J. Finneran; copyright © 1924 by The Macmillan Company; copyright renewed 1952 by Georgie Yeats. "Sailing to Byzantium" and "The Stare's Nest by My Window" are reprinted the permission of Scribner, an imprint of Simon & Schuster Adult Publishing Group, from *The Complete Works of W. B. Yeats: Volume I, The Poems, Revised*, edited by Richard J. Finneran; copyright © 1928 by The Macmillan Company; copyright renewed 1956 by Georgie Yeats. All other poems in this volume are reprinted with the permission of Scribner, an imprint of Simon & Schuster Adult Publishing Group, from *The Complete Works of W. B. Yeats: Volume I, The Poems, Revised*, edited by Richard J. Finneran (New York: Scribner, 1996).

4 6 8 10 9 7 5

Published by Sterling Publishing Co., Inc.
387 Park Avenue South, New York, N.Y. 10016
Text © 2002 by Jonathan Allison
Illustrations © 2002 by Glenn Harrington
Distributed in Canada by Sterling Publishing
℅ Canadian Manda Group, 165 Dufferin Street
Toronto, Ontario, Canada M6K 3H6
Distributed in Great Britain by Chrysalis Books Group PLC
The Chrysalis Building, Bramley Road, London W10 6SP, England
Distributed in Australia by Capricorn Link (Australia) Pty Ltd.
P.O. Box 704, Windsor, NSW 2756 Australia

Sterling ISBN 0-8069-6615-7

For information about custom editions, special sales, premium and corporate purchases, please contact
Sterling Special Sales Department at 800-805-5489 or specialsales@sterlingpub.com

CONTENTS

INTRODUCTION

Not only was William Butler Yeats a great poet—perhaps the finest modern poet in the English language—but he was other things too: a playwright, a theatre manager, a patriot, a senator, and a believer in fairies and ghosts.

Born in Dublin on June 13, 1865, Yeats was called "Willie" by his family, but many others called him "WB." He was the oldest of six children, all of them dark and good-looking. WB was particularly close to his sister Susan (she was called Lily), who was a year younger than he was. She and her younger sister, Lolly (her real name was Elizabeth), were both very artistic and grew up to found "Dun Emer Industries," a company renowned for embroidery and fine printing; they printed many editions of their brother's books. A younger brother, Jack (born 1871), was independent, good-humored, and very talented. He grew up to become one of Ireland's greatest painters.

WB's father, John Butler Yeats, was a powerful personality who had a huge influence on his children. Often he would read poems and stories to them from the works of Chaucer, Shakespeare, Sir Walter Scott, and others. He had been trained as a lawyer, but soon decided that he wanted to be an artist, went to art school, and became a well-known portrait painter.

Susan Pollexfen, WB's mother, was a quiet, withdrawn woman, the daughter of a well-to-do shipping family in Sligo. Always prone to depression, she was deeply affected by the death in 1873 of her son Robert, at the age of three. She fell into a despondency from which she never fully recovered. Before young Robert's death, she claims she heard the call of the "banshee," a wailing ghost of Irish folklore, who is said to prophesy the imminent death of a loved one.

When Yeats was two, his family moved to London, returning to Sligo for their summer holidays, but between the ages of seven and nine, WB lived in Sligo with his mother at "Merville," the home of her parents. Her father owned a fleet of merchant ships, and WB would watch them on the river as they voyaged to and from England.

A firm believer in ghosts and spooks, WB claims he first saw a fairy at Merville. In Ireland in those days, many people—especially country people—believed implicitly in the supernatural, and there would have been much talk of it among the servants at Merville. These fairies were not the kind, loving sort you might see in a movie, but were often treacherous and dangerous. As you can see in a poem like "The Stolen Child" (page 10), based on a popular legend, it was believed that fairies could kidnap you and force you to live with them. In "The Hosting of the Sidhe" (page 16), the poet imagines a vast number of fairies or "sidhe" (pronounced "shee") riding on horseback across the land.

There was a pony at Merville, and several dogs with which the children chased rabbits. As a child, WB was a keen naturalist, particularly fond of moths, butterflies, beetles, and newts, which he occasionally collected in glass jars. He used to go rowing and sailing with his uncle in Rosses Point, a small seaside town close to Sligo, and he would fish for pike and trout in nearby rivers and lakes. Sometimes he would go fishing for mackerel in the sea at Sligo Bay.

The young Yeats went on long walks in the Sligo countryside and sometimes spent the night in caves in the woods. You can see his love for the area in many of his poems, which often mention local place names and landmarks, such as Ben Bulben, Knocknarea, Sleuth Wood, Glen-Car, and Dooney (see "The Fiddler of Dooney," page 24).

Yeats was not a particularly gifted student at school—he had great difficulty with spelling, for example—but he began writing poetry at about age fifteen. His earliest poems, about witches and medieval knights in armor, were not very original, but his verse began to come alive when he wrote about Irish legends and myths, such as those of the folk hero Cuchulain, who was said to have superhuman powers. WB published his first poems in a Dublin magazine when he was twenty.

Also in his twentieth year, Yeats began attending a Dublin club where members discussed the political issues of the day, including that of Irish independence from Britain. WB wanted to work for political freedom, too, but through artistic and cultural means, not by spending his life on committees.

Ever since the days at Merville, Yeats had been intrigued with the mystical, the paranormal, and the occult. At the age of twenty he helped to found the Dublin Hermetic Society ("hermetic" means "magical"), a group of students devoted to studying Indian philosophy and mysticism. This club later became The Dublin Theosophical Society ("theosophy" means "divine wisdom"). He attended his first séance the following year and later joined the Order of the Golden Dawn, a secret society that promoted the study and practice of ritual magic. For much of his life, especially when young, Yeats was fascinated by séances, telepathy, and astral projection, and he spent a great deal of time having visions or trying to have visions of the supernatural. These interests are reflected in his poetry, early and late. The occult was very important to Yeats. Once, when challenged, he retorted that the occult was at the center of all that he did and thought.

In 1889, at the age of twenty-three, he met and fell in love with a beautiful actress called Maud Gonne, a revolutionary and a political firebrand. For many years they were the closest of friends. Most of his love poems are addressed to her, including two printed here: "The Fish" (page 18) and "He Wishes for the Cloths of Heaven" (page 22). He proposed marriage to her several times, but she repeatedly turned him down. In 1903, she married the Irish soldier, Major John MacBride, who was later executed for his part in the Irish rebellion of 1916.

WB was also a playwright. In 1899 he founded, with playwright and friend Lady Gregory, the Irish Literary Theatre. Its aim was to put on plays based on Irish subject matter and life. Many of the plays they staged, such as Yeats's *The Countess Kathleen* and *Cathleen ni Houlihan* (in which Maud Gonne played the leading role) were fiercely patriotic. A few years later, he established the famous Abbey Theatre in Dublin, which survives to this day.

In 1911, WB met for the first time, at the home of a friend, a tall, pretty young woman called Georgie Hyde-Lees. Then only eighteen years old, she was a voracious reader, fluent in several languages, and interested in the occult. Soon, she too joined the Order of the Golden Dawn. Although a romance did not begin at this time, they later courted and were married in 1917. In that year, Yeats bought and had restored an old Norman tower in Ballylee, County Galway, where he lived with Georgie during the summer. He wrote many poems there, including this one: "To be carved on a stone at Thoor Ballylee":

> I, the poet William Yeats,
> With old mill boards and sea-green slates,
> And smithy work from the Gort forge,
> Restored this tower for my wife George;
> And may these characters remain
> When all is ruin once again.

Shortly after Yeats was married, he believed he had established contact with various spiritual instructors and guides, working through his wife as a medium. The sometimes garbled messages, delivered through Georgie's "automatic writing," performed in a trancelike state, formed the basis of his strange and mysterious book, *A Vision*.

The couple had two children, Anne Butler Yeats, born 1919, who became an artist, and Michael Butler Yeats, born 1921, who chose a career in politics and became, like his father, a member of the Irish Senate.

There was a rebellion in Ireland in 1916, in which hundreds of people, including some of Yeats's friends, were killed. Finally, the rebels surrendered and the British army stationed in Ireland executed the leaders. Later, war broke out between the Irish rebels and British forces. This lasted for two years. A treaty was signed, but then civil war began between those who accepted the treaty and those who did not. "Meditations in Time of Civil War" (page 46), a sequence of seven poems, was written during this period.

Yeats served as a Senator in the first Irish Government, from 1922 to 1928, and worked hard to preserve Ireland's rich cultural heritage—its architecture, ancient monuments, and manuscripts. He opposed censorship, fought for artistic freedom, and tried to improve the condition of Irish schools. While leading a committee to design new coins, he insisted that they reflect the agricultural economy of the nation. The coins showed a horse, a salmon, a pig, a bull, a chicken, a dog, and a rabbit. Until the introduction of the Euro in 2002, Irish coins in circulation continued to display these animal designs. It was during this time, in 1923, that he was awarded the Nobel Prize for literature.

W.B. Yeats continued writing until he died in 1939 at the age of seventy-three. He was then living in the south of France, where he spent a good deal of time in his old age, partly for health reasons. Georgie lived on until 1968. Though buried in France, WB's body was removed at the end of World War Two, transported to Ireland, and buried in 1948 in Drumcliffe churchyard, near Sligo. Under the mighty mountain, Ben Bulben ("Ben" is the Irish word for peak or mountain), the tombstone bears the poet's epitaph, lines taken from his great poem, "Under Ben Bulben":

"Cast a cold eye
On life, on death.
Horseman, pass by!"

THE SAD SHEPHERD

The shepherd knows Sorrow so well that it calls him a friend.
He talks aloud to the stars, the sea, and the dewdrops, but
this does not help. Finally, he tells his sad story to a seashell.
His words and thoughts in the poem are printed in italics.

There was a man whom Sorrow named his friend,
And he, of his high comrade Sorrow dreaming,
Went walking with slow steps along the gleaming
And humming sands, where windy surges wend:
And he called loudly to the stars to bend
From their pale thrones and comfort him, but they
Among themselves laugh on and sing alway:
And then the man whom Sorrow named his friend
Cried out, *Dim sea, hear my most piteous story!*
The sea swept on and cried her old cry still,
Rolling along in dreams from hill to hill.
He fled the persecution of her glory
And, in a far-off, gentle valley stopping,
Cried all his story to the dewdrops glistening.
But naught they heard, for they are always listening,
The dewdrops, for the sound of their own dropping.
And then the man whom Sorrow named his friend
Sought once again the shore, and found a shell,
And thought, *I will my heavy story tell*
Till my own words, re-echoing, shall send
Their sadness through a hollow, pearly heart;
And my own tale again for me shall sing,
And my own whispering words be comforting,
And lo! my ancient burden may depart.
Then he sang softly nigh the pearly rim;
But the sad dweller by the sea-ways lone
Changed all he sang to inarticulate moan
Among her wildering whirls, forgetting him.

high comrade—*noble and distinguished friend*
surges—*waves*
piteous—*pitiful*

fled the persecution of her glory—
fled the sea, whose indifference to
his plight felt hurtful

heavy story—*sad story*
nigh—*near*
pearly rim—*lip of the shell*

sad dweller—*the shell*
inarticulate—*not spoken clearly*
wildering—*bewildering*

9

THE STOLEN CHILD

In Irish folklore, it was said that fairies sometimes came in the night to steal children from their homes and enslave them in fairyland. In this poem, the fairies themselves speak to the reader. As we often find in Yeats's poetry, there are several references to places in County Sligo, Ireland. He spent many happy summers there in his youth.

Where dips the rocky highland
Of Sleuth Wood in the lake,
There lies a leafy island
Where flapping herons wake
The drowsy water-rats;
There we've hid our faery vats,
Full of berries
And of reddest stolen cherries.
Come away, O human child!
To the waters and the wild
With a faery, hand in hand,
For the world's more full of weeping
  than you can understand.

Where the wave of moonlight glosses
The dim grey sands with light,
Far off by furthest Rosses
We foot it all the night,
Weaving olden dances,
Mingling hands and mingling glances
Till the moon has taken flight;
To and fro we leap
And chase the frothy bubbles,
While the world is full of troubles
And is anxious in its sleep.
Come away, O human child!
To the waters and the wild
With a faery, hand in hand,
For the world's more full of weeping
  than you can understand.

highland—*high ground*
Sleuth Wood—*also known as Slish Wood, on the edge of Lough Gill,*
  County Sligo
herons—*large wading birds*
vats—*large vessels, urns*
glosses—*illuminates the wet sand*
Rosses—*Rosses Point, seaside town near the town of Sligo*

Where the wandering water gushes
From the hills above Glen-Car,
In pools among the rushes
That scarce could bathe a star,
We seek for slumbering trout
And whispering in their ears
Give them unquiet dreams;
Leaning softly out
From ferns that drop their tears
Over the young streams.
Come away, O human child!
To the waters and the wild
With a faery, hand in hand,
For the world's more full of weeping
    than you can understand.

Away with us he's going,
The solemn-eyed:
He'll hear no more the lowing
Of the calves on the warm hillside
Or the kettle on the hob
Sing peace into his breast,
Or see the brown mice bob
Round and round the oatmeal-chest.
For he comes, the human child,
To the waters and the wild
With a faery, hand in hand,
From a world more full of weeping
    than he can understand.

Glen-Car—*glen of the standing stone,*
    county Sligo, where there is a lake and a
    waterfall
rushes—*grasslike plants that grow in*
    marshes and pools
lowing—*sound made by cattle*
hob—*hot surface beside a fireplace*

THE MEDITATION OF THE OLD FISHERMAN

Yeats claimed that this poem was based on a conversation with a fisherman in Sligo. Now an old man, the fisherman contrasts the present with his fondly remembered boyhood.

You waves, though you dance by my feet like children at play,
Though you glow and you glance, though you purr and you dart;
In the Junes that were warmer than these are, the waves were more gay,
When I was a boy with never a crack in my heart.

The herring are not in the tides as they were of old;
My sorrow! for many a creak gave the creel in the cart
That carried the take to Sligo town to be sold,
When I was a boy with never a crack in my heart.

And ah, you proud maiden, you are not so fair when his oar
Is heard on the water, as they were, the proud and apart,
Who paced in the eve by the nets on the pebbly shore,
When I was a boy with never a crack in my heart.

never a crack in my heart—*when young,
    carefree, and innocent*
creel—*wicker basket*
the take—*the catch*

12

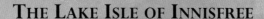

THE LAKE ISLE OF INNISFREE

The idea for this poem came to Yeats as he was standing in a bustling London street. He thought of County Sligo, where he had often stayed with relatives in his youth. He imagines going to live in a cabin on that peaceful, little island.

I will arise and go now, and go to Innisfree,
And a small cabin build there, of clay and wattles made:
Nine bean-rows will I have there, a hive for the honey-bee,
And live alone in the bee-loud glade.

And I shall have some peace there, for peace comes dropping slow,
Dropping from the veils of the morning to where the cricket sings;
There midnight's all a glimmer, and noon a purple glow,
And evening full of the linnet's wings.

I will arise and go now, for always night and day
I hear lake water lapping with low sounds by the shore;
While I stand on the roadway, or on the pavements grey,
I hear it in the deep heart's core.

Innisfree—*from the Irish, "the heathery island," a*
    small island in Lough Gill, County Sligo
wattles—*rods and branches interwoven*
glade—*open space in a wood*
purple glow—*appearance of the purple heather*
    in sunlight
linnet—*small bird*

TO SOME I HAVE TALKED WITH BY THE FIRE

In this very mysterious poem, the poet remembers fireside conversations he used to have with his friends about spirits, angels, and other supernatural beings, such as "twilight companies" and the "flaming multitude." The poem ends with the coming of the dawn.

While I wrought out these fitful Danaan rhymes,
My heart would brim with dreams about the times
When we bent down above the fading coals
And talked of the dark folk who live in souls
Of passionate men, like bats in the dead trees;
And of the wayward twilight companies
Who sigh with mingled sorrow and content,
Because their blossoming dreams have never bent
Under the fruit of evil and of good:
And of the embattled flaming multitude
Who rise, wing above wing, flame above flame,
And, like a storm, cry the Ineffable Name,
And with the clashing of their sword-blades make
A rapturous music, till the morning break
And the white hush end all but the loud beat
Of their long wings, the flash of their white feet.

wrought—*made, wrote*
fitful—*irregular*
Danaan—*of the Tuatha de Danaan, legendary magical inhabitants of*
   Ireland
wayward—*willful and changeable*
embattled—*ready for battle or engaged in battle*
Ineffable Name—*inexpressible name such as that of a god*
rapturous—*delightful and passionate*

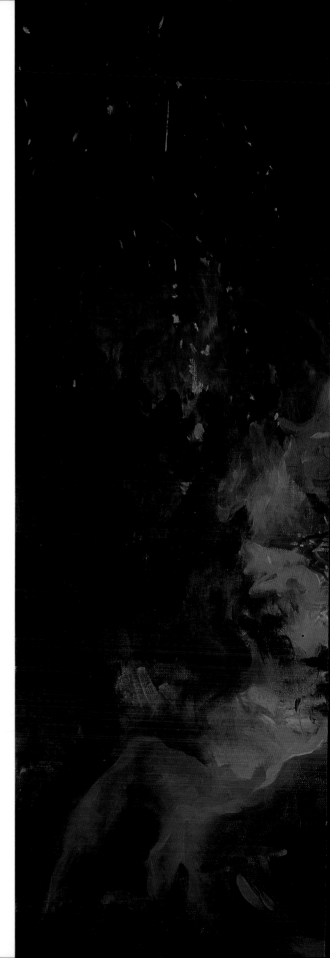

THE HOSTING OF THE SIDHE

The poet imagines the fairies of Ireland galloping on horseback across the landscape of County Sligo. The fairy princess Niamh speaks for them. Yeats originally called the poem "The Faery Host." When you read it aloud, you'll find that its beat is like the regular rhythm of galloping horses.

The host is riding from Knocknarea
And over the grave of Clooth-na-Bare;
Caoilte tossing his burning hair,
And Niamh calling *Away, come away:*
Empty your heart of its mortal dream.
The winds awaken, the leaves whirl round,
Our cheeks are pale, our hair is unbound,
Our breasts are heaving, our eyes are agleam,
Our arms are waving, our lips are apart;
And if any gaze on our rushing band,
We come between him and the deed of his hand,
We come between him and the hope of his heart.
The host is rushing 'twixt night and day,
And where is there hope or deed as fair?
Caoilte tossing his burning hair,
And Niamh calling *Away, come away.*

Sidhe—*pronounced Shee. Irish fairies, who were thought to travel in the wind*
Knocknarea—*pronounced Nock-na-ray. A mountain near the town of Sligo*
Clooth-na-Bare—*legendary fairy woman who drowned herself in a deep lake*
Caoilte—*pronounced Keel-chih, a legendary warrior*
Niamh—*pronounced Nee-iv, a fairy princess who lured Oisin (pronounced Osheen), a legendary warrior and poet, to a magical land for 300 years*

THE FISH

Seemingly addressing his words to a fish, who hides in the water and leaps out of the fisherman's net, the speaker is really talking about a person who is running away from him, and about how difficult it can be to make someone love you. At the end, the speaker says that in future people will judge her harshly for continually escaping him.

Although you hide in the ebb and flow
Of the pale tide when the moon has set,
The people of coming days will know
About the casting out of my net,
And how you have leaped times out of mind
Over the little silver cords,
And think that you were hard and unkind,
And blame you with many bitter words.

THE SONG OF WANDERING AENGUS

Yeats claimed that a Greek folk song inspired this poem, and that there were many similarities between Greek and Irish legends. At the end of the poem, Aengus is on a quest to locate the magical girl who was changed from a fish into a human being—but she is very hard to find.

I went out to the hazel wood,
Because a fire was in my head,
And cut and peeled a hazel wand,
And hooked a berry to a thread;
And when white moths were on the wing,
And moth-like stars were flickering out,
I dropped the berry in a stream
And caught a little silver trout.

When I had laid it on the floor
I went to blow the fire aflame,
But something rustled on the floor,
And some one called me by my name:
It had become a glimmering girl
With apple blossom in her hair
Who called me by my name and ran
And faded through the brightening air.

Though I am old with wandering
Through hollow lands and hilly lands,
I will find out where she has gone,
And kiss her lips and take her hands;
And walk among long dappled grass,
And pluck till time and times are done
The silver apples of the moon,
The golden apples of the sun.

Aengus—*legendary god of love, youth, and poetry*
hazel wood—*wood near Lough Gill in County Sligo*
dappled—*spotted or mottled*
silver apples—*apples that appear silvery white by
   moonlight*

THE VALLEY OF THE BLACK PIG

In this vision of a fierce and terrible battle, seen in a dream, Yeats imagines spears, warriors on horseback, and the shouts and cries of the fallen. Finally, the poem ends peacefully, with a prayer to a god or divine being.

The dews drop slowly and dreams gather: unknown spears
Suddenly hurtle before my dream-awakened eyes,
And then the clash of fallen horsemen and the cries
Of unknown perishing armies beat about my ears.
We who still labour by the cromlech on the shore,
The grey cairn on the hill, when day sinks drowned in dew,
Being weary of the world's empires, bow down to you,
Master of the still stars and of the flaming door.

Valley of the Black Pig—*legendary site of a great Irish battle that has been foretold*
cromlech—*stone circle, possibly an ancient burial site*
cairn—*a heap of stones marking an ancient grave, such as the one atop Knocknarea*
flaming door—*possibly a doorway to eternity*

HE WISHES FOR THE CLOTHS OF HEAVEN

Yeats imagines the sky as a vast cloth, stitched with light from the sun, moon, and stars. He says he would like to roll out this vast cloth as a carpet for the feet of the woman he loves, but all he can afford is a carpet of dreams. Many readers will understand the poet's fear of someone walking all over his hopes and dreams.

Had I the heavens' embroidered cloths,
Enwrought with golden and silver light,
The blue and the dim and the dark cloths
Of night and light and the half-light,
I would spread the cloths under your feet:
But I, being poor, have only my dreams;
I have spread my dreams under your feet;
Tread softly because you tread on my dreams.

enwrought—*sewn or embroidered*
tread—*walk*

22

THE FIDDLER OF DOONEY

*The fiddler of Dooney loves to play his music and watch people dance to it.
He mentions that his brother and cousin are both priests, but he himself
prefers fiddling his songs to saying his prayers. The jaunty beat or rhythm of
the verse suits the theme of joyful music and dancing.*

When I play on my fiddle in Dooney,
Folk dance like a wave of the sea;
My cousin is priest in Kilvarnet,
My brother in Mocharabuiee.

I passed my brother and cousin:
They read in their books of prayer;
I read in my book of songs
I bought at the Sligo fair.

When we come at the end of time
To Peter sitting in state,
He will smile on the three old spirits,
But call me first through the gate;

For the good are always the merry,
Save by an evil chance,
And the merry love the fiddle,
And the merry love to dance:

And when the folk there spy me,
They will all come up to me,
With 'Here is the fiddler of Dooney!'
And dance like a wave of the sea.

Dooney—*Dooney Rock, on the shore of Lough Gill. A popular spot for outdoor
    dancing*
Kilvarnet—*A tiny village in County Sligo with an old ruined church*
Mocharabuiee—*Pronounced Mock-rabwee, a village in County Sligo*
Peter—*Saint Peter, at the gates of Heaven*

THE OLD MEN ADMIRING THEMSELVES IN THE WATER

The hands and legs of the old men are twisted and bent, but this sad and thoughtful poem about the passage of time ends with a note of acceptance and resignation toward growing old.

I heard the old, old men say,
'Everything alters,
And one by one we drop away.'
They had hands like claws, and their knees
Were twisted like the old thorn-trees
By the waters.
I heard the old, old men say,
'All that's beautiful drifts away
Like the waters.'

thorn-trees—*thorny trees, such as hawthorn*

AT GALWAY RACES

At a famous racecourse in the west of Ireland, the poet admires the jockeys on horseback and enjoys the general atmosphere of the races. He wishes that the audience for his poems was as large and enthusiastic as the audience for horse racing, as he believes it used to be. He hopes one day people will wake up and recover their lost passion for poetry and for life.

There where the course is,
Delight makes all of the one mind,
The riders upon the galloping horses,
The crowd that closes in behind:
We, too, had good attendance once,
Hearers and hearteners of the work;
Aye, horsemen for companions,
Before the merchant and the clerk
Breathed on the world with timid breath.
Sing on: somewhere at some new moon,
We'll learn that sleeping is not death,
Hearing the whole earth change its tune,
Its flesh being wild, and it again
Crying aloud as the racecourse is,
And we find hearteners among men
That ride upon horses.

hearteners—*encouraging friends, supporters*

RUNNING TO PARADISE

The speaker is a penniless beggar who is very lively and carefree, despite his poverty. He is happy with the occasional coins and scraps of food people throw to him. He compares his life to that of his wealthier brother, and in the refrain (the repeated line at the end of each stanza or verse), he claims that, in Paradise, the beggar is the equal of the king. Finally, he says that his best friend is the wind itself, because it is completely free and cannot be bought or tied down.

As I came over Windy Gap
They threw a halfpenny into my cap,
For I am running to Paradise;
And all that I need do is to wish
And somebody puts his hand in the dish
To throw me a bit of salted fish:
And there the king is but as the beggar.

My brother Mourteen is worn out
With skelping his big brawling lout,
And I am running to Paradise;
A poor life, do what he can,
And though he keep a dog and a gun,
A serving-maid and a serving-man:
And there the king is but as the beggar.

Poor men have grown to be rich men,
And rich men grown to be poor again,
And I am running to Paradise;
And many a darling wit's grown dull
That tossed a bare heel when at school,
Now it has filled an old sock full:
And there the king is but as the beggar.

The wind is old and still at play
While I must hurry upon my way,
For I am running to Paradise;
Yet never have I lit on a friend
To take my fancy like the wind
That nobody can buy or bind:
And there the king is but as the beggar.

Windy Gap—*there are several places called this in the west of Ireland*
skelping—*beating or hitting*
darling wit—*lively, jovial person*
tossed a bare heel—*suggests carefree and barefooted poverty*
old sock full—*sign of wealth; a sockful of money*
lit on—*found*

TO A CHILD DANCING IN THE WIND

Yeats views the carefree innocence of childhood—
from an adult point of view.

Dance there upon the shore;
What need have you to care
For wind or water's roar?
And tumble out your hair
That the salt drops have wet;
Being young you have not known
The fool's triumph, nor yet
Love lost as soon as won,
Nor the best labourer dead
And all the sheaves to bind.
What need have you to dread
The monstrous crying of wind?

all the sheaves to bind—*sheaves of hay to gather in*
from the field and tie

A COAT

There are many styles of poetry; Yeats talks about two of them here: an elaborate style with mythological references, like a richly embroidered tapestry or coat, and a plain, simple style, which he compares to a naked man. The poet decides that, in future, he will adopt the more simple, "naked" style.

I made my song a coat
Covered with embroideries
Out of old mythologies
From heel to throat;
But the fools caught it,
Wore it in the world's eyes
As though they'd wrought it.
Song, let them take it,
For there's more enterprise
In walking naked.

wrought—*made*
there's more enterprise—*it is bolder*
   and more profitable

THE WILD SWANS AT COOLE

Coole Park was a large estate in County Galway, Ireland, where Yeats used to visit his friend, the playwright Lady Gregory. He wrote many poems there, including this one. Now over 50 years of age, and beginning to feel rather old, he recalls his first visit to Coole, 19 years earlier, when he first saw the startling display of wild swans as they lifted off all at once from the lake.

The trees are in their autumn beauty,
The woodland paths are dry,
Under the October twilight the water
Mirrors a still sky;
Upon the brimming water among the stones
Are nine-and-fifty swans.

The nineteenth autumn has come upon me
Since I first made my count;
I saw, before I had well finished,
All suddenly mount
And scatter wheeling in great broken rings
Upon their clamorous wings.

I have looked upon those brilliant creatures,
And now my heart is sore.
All's changed since I, hearing at twilight,
The first time on this shore,
The bell-beat of their wings above my head,
Trod with a lighter tread.

Unwearied still, lover by lover,
They paddle in the cold
Companionable streams or climb the air;
Their hearts have not grown old;
Passion or conquest, wander where they will,
Attend upon them still.

But now they drift on the still water,
Mysterious, beautiful;
Among what rushes will they build,
By what lake's edge or pool
Delight men's eyes when I awake some day
To find they have flown away?

clamorous—*noisy*

AN IRISH AIRMAN FORESEES HIS DEATH

Lady Gregory's son, Major Robert Gregory, was an Irish pilot who served in the British Air Force, in World War One. He was killed in action. In this tribute to him, the speaker explains his feelings of courage, calm, and strange excitement, prior to a dangerous flying mission "among the clouds above."

I know that I shall meet my fate
Somewhere among the clouds above;
Those that I fight I do not hate,
Those that I guard I do not love;
My country is Kiltartan Cross,
My countrymen Kiltartan's poor,
No likely end could bring them loss
Or leave them happier than before.
Nor law, nor duty bade me fight,
Nor public men, nor cheering crowds,
A lonely impulse of delight
Drove to this tumult in the clouds;
I balanced all, brought all to mind,
The years to come seemed waste of breath,
A waste of breath the years behind
In balance with this life, this death.

Those that I fight—*the Germans*
Those that I guard—*the British*
Kiltartan Cross—*a place near Coole Park, County Galway*
tumult—*state of noisy commotion and emotional disturbance*

THE BALLOON OF THE MIND

Think of the ways in which your own mind is like a big, floating balloon, and how you sometimes have to drag it down into a confined space!

Hands, do what you're bid:
Bring the balloon of the mind
That bellies and drags in the wind
Into its narrow shed.

TO A SQUIRREL AT KYLE-NA-NO

The Irish language place-name "Kyle-na-no" means the wood of nuts. It is one of the seven woods at Coole Park, the home of Lady Gregory. The speaker tries to reassure the squirrel that he is friendly.

Come play with me;
Why should you run
Through the shaking tree
As though I'd a gun
To strike you dead?
When all I would do
Is to scratch your head
And let you go.

THE HAWK

In an earlier poem, Yeats looked at the mind as a balloon, but here he views the mind as a hawk. He usually associates the hawk with the straight path of logic and the butterfly with the crooked path of intuition. The poem has three different speakers—one in each verse. The first wants to control the hawk; the second shows the hawk's reply to that. In the third, the poet scolds himself for appearing silly while talking to a friend. He addresses the hawk, but it is as if he is talking to himself.

'Call down the hawk from the air;
Let him be hooded or caged
Till the yellow eye has grown mild,
For larder and spit are bare,
The old cook enraged,
The scullion gone wild.'

'I will not be clapped in a hood,
Nor a cage, nor alight upon wrist,
Now I have learnt to be proud
Hovering over the wood
In the broken mist
Or tumbling cloud.'

'What tumbling cloud did you cleave,
Yellow-eyed hawk of the mind,
Last evening? that I, who had sat
Dumbfounded before a knave,
Should give to my friend
A pretence of wit.'

hooded—*falconers put little hoods on hawks to train
   and calm them*
larder—*pantry*
scullion—*servant*
cleave—*cut through*
knave—*fool*

THE CAT AND THE MOON

The cat, called Minnaloushe, is fascinated by the moon, portrayed here as a close relative of the cat. Just as the moon changes shape from full to new moon, so do the pupils of the cat's eyes. The poet imagines the cat slowly dancing in the moonlight.

The cat went here and there
And the moon spun round like a top,
And the nearest kin of the moon,
The creeping cat, looked up.
Black Minnaloushe stared at the moon,
For, wander and wail as he would,
The pure cold light in the sky
Troubled his animal blood.
Minnaloushe runs in the grass
Lifting his delicate feet.
Do you dance, Minnaloushe, do you dance?
When two close kindred meet,
What better than call a dance?
Maybe the moon may learn,
Tired of that courtly fashion,
A new dance turn.
Minnaloushe creeps through the grass
From moonlit place to place,
The sacred moon overhead
Has taken a new phase.
Does Minnaloushe know that his pupils
Will pass from change to change,
And that from round to crescent,
From crescent to round they range?
Minnaloushe creeps through the grass
Alone, important and wise,
And lifts to the changing moon
His changing eyes.

TWO SONGS OF A FOOL

Poets often think of poems as musical and song-like, because they have rhyme and regular rhythm, as songs do. These poems tell of a kind man who lives with a pet cat and a hare. He blames himself because the hare escapes and runs away while he is sleeping. Try reading the poems as if the cat and hare were not animals, but real people who were friends of the poet.

I

A speckled cat and a tame hare
Eat at my hearthstone
And sleep there;
And both look up to me alone
For learning and defence
As I look up to Providence.

I start out of my sleep to think
Some day I may forget
Their food and drink;
Or, the house door left unshut,
The hare may run till it's found
The horn's sweet note and the tooth of the hound.

I bear a burden that might well try
Men that do all by rule,
And what can I
That am a wandering-witted fool
But pray to God that He ease
My great responsibilities?

II

I slept on my three-legged stool by the fire,
The speckled cat slept on my knee;
We never thought to enquire
Where the brown hare might be,
And whether the door were shut.
Who knows how she drank the wind
Stretched up on two legs from the mat,
Before she had settled her mind
To drum with her heel and to leap?
Had I but awakened from sleep
And called her name, she had heard,
It may be, and had not stirred,
That now, it may be, has found
The horn's sweet note and the tooth of the hound.

hearthstone—*fireplace*   Providence—*God or Fate*   the horn's sweet note—*the sound of the hunter's horn*

THE SECOND COMING

While the title of this visionary poem suggests the second coming of Jesus Christ, as foretold in the Bible, the poem actually deals with something very different. As in "The Valley of the Black Pig," the poet has a vision of terrible events in the future. He fears that the world will be plunged into chaos and bloodshed. He also has a frightening vision of a "rough beast," rather like a sphinx, waking up in the desert, and plodding slowly towards Bethlehem to be born. If the birth of Jesus led to the spread of Christianity, what sort of world will it be after the birth of this savage creature?

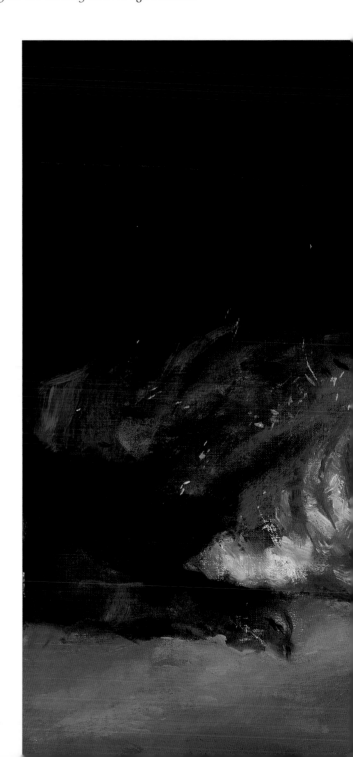

Turning and turning in the widening gyre
The falcon cannot hear the falconer;
Things fall apart; the centre cannot hold;
Mere anarchy is loosed upon the world,
The blood-dimmed tide is loosed, and everywhere
The ceremony of innocence is drowned;
The best lack all conviction, while the worst
Are full of passionate intensity.

Surely some revelation is at hand;
Surely the Second Coming is at hand.
The Second Coming! Hardly are those words out
When a vast image out of *Spiritus Mundi*
Troubles my sight: somewhere in sands of the desert
A shape with lion body and the head of a man,
A gaze blank and pitiless as the sun,
Is moving its slow thighs, while all about it
Reel shadows of the indignant desert birds.
The darkness drops again; but now I know
That twenty centuries of stony sleep
Were vexed to nightmare by a rocking cradle,
And what rough beast, its hour come round at last,
Slouches towards Bethlehem to be born?

gyre—*spiraling circle, suggesting the passage of time*

anarchy—*state of extreme disorder*

blood-dimmed tide—*implies widespread bloodshed*

revelation—*enlightening experience*

Spiritus Mundi—*from Latin, "spirit of the world." Yeats believed in the existence of a big spiritual storehouse containing many images, visions, and prophecies, which certain people could gain access to*

shape with lion body—*sphinx*

SAILING TO BYZANTIUM

Faced with the prospect of growing old, the poet wishes he could turn himself into a golden bird with the power of prophecy, sitting on a branch in the ancient capital of eastern Christianity, Byzantium. The poet contrasts natural life, which does not last forever, with everlasting art, and its "monuments of unageing intellect"—monuments such as this poem. He asks the saints and wise men depicted on the walls of Byzantine churches to help him to escape his dying body and enter into eternity.

I

That is no country for old men. The young
In one another's arms, birds in the trees
—Those dying generations—at their song,
The salmon-falls, the mackerel-crowded seas,
Fish, flesh, or fowl, commend all summer long
Whatever is begotten, born, and dies.
Caught in that sensual music all neglect
Monuments of unageing intellect.

II

An aged man is but a paltry thing,
A tattered coat upon a stick, unless
Soul clap its hands and sing, and louder sing
For every tatter in its mortal dress,
Nor is there singing school but studying
Monuments of its own magnificence;
And therefore I have sailed the seas and come
To the holy city of Byzantium.

dying generations—*people, birds, and all mortal creatures*
sensual music—*world of the senses*
paltry—*worthless, trashy*
Byzantium—*ancient city, later called Constantinople, now Istanbul*

III

O sages standing in God's holy fire
As in the gold mosaic of a wall,
Come from the holy fire, perne in a gyre,
And be the singing-masters of my soul.
Consume my heart away; sick with desire
And fastened to a dying animal
It knows not what it is; and gather me
Into the artifice of eternity.

IV

Once out of nature I shall never take
My bodily form from any natural thing,
But such a form as Grecian goldsmiths make
Of hammered gold and gold enamelling
To keep a drowsy Emperor awake;
Or set upon a golden bough to sing
To lords and ladies of Byzantium
Of what is past, or passing, or to come.

sages—*saints, such as those depicted on church mosaics*
perne in a gyre—*twist and spin through time*
artifice—*artwork*

THE STARE'S NEST BY MY WINDOW

The sixth in a sequence of poems titled
"Meditations in Time of Civil War," the following
poem was written in 1922, in the midst of terrible
warfare in Ireland. Here, with death and bloodshed
as background, he concentrates on the beauty of
the honey-bees that he invites to build in his
walls.

The bees build in the crevices
Of loosening masonry, and there
The mother birds bring grubs and flies.
My wall is loosening; honey-bees,
Come build in the empty house of the stare.

We are closed in, and the key is turned
On our uncertainty; somewhere
A man is killed, or a house burned,
Yet no clear fact to be discerned:
Come build in the empty house of the stare.

A barricade of stone or of wood;
Some fourteen days of civil war;
Last night they trundled down the road
That dead young soldier in his blood:
Come build in the empty house of the stare.

We had fed the heart on fantasies,
The heart's grown brutal from the fare;
More substance in our enmities
Than in our love; O honey-bees,
Come build in the empty house of the stare.

stare—*starling*

crevices—*cracks*

masonry—*stone wall*

discerned—*made out or understood*

trundled—*carried by cart or car*

the fare—*food*

enmities—*hatred*

INDEX